ON THE

OTHER

SIDE

OF

YOUR PAIN

Hope For The Hurting

Terri Jordan

True Potential
REACH THE WORLD

All Scripture quotations, unless otherwise noted, are from the New King James Version of the Bible. Copyright © 1982 by Thomas Nelson, Inc. Used by permission. All rights reserved.

On The Other Side Of Your Pain: Hope For The Hurting

Cover and Interior Page design by True Potential, Inc.

ISBN: (Paperback): 9781960024732

ISBN: (e-book): 9781960024749

LCCN: 2025938950

True Potential

REACH THE WORLD

True Potential, Inc.
PO Box 904, Travelers Rest, SC 29690
www.truepotentialmedia.com
Cover and Interior Page design by True Potential, Inc.

DEDICATION

This book is dedicated to all of you out there who have a desire to make a change in your life. Those who are willing to face the truth head on and tackle the situation with a brave heart.

You deserve to be recognized because you have put aside the fears of failure and ridicule. You've made a decision to do whatever it takes to become who you truly are deep inside.

I am proud of you, and I feel confident in saying that every other person who has read this book is also proud of you. There is hope no matter what things may currently look like.

You matter! Your presence in this world matters... you truly make a difference.

Now, take the leap of faith required to successfully arrive on the other side of your pain. Take one step at a time, but take that step. The journey is shorter than you think. The end result is a brand new you with a brand new life! I believe in you!

ACKNOWLEDGMENTS

When I began to realize this book has a huge probability of being in the hands of someone who is seeking a solution for their hurt and pain, I paused for a moment and wished them great peace. Truly, we never know whose life we may impact on the other side of our pain. That is why we must push forward and never give up. **However, without forgiveness we will never really heal.** The power of forgiveness extends beyond the boundaries we have quietly built. Tearing down those boundaries happens when we quietly allow love to grow. In this place lies your freedom!

Therefore, I acknowledge the trials I have endured and the times I felt all alone in this world, and I give thanks. Without those trials, I would not be here writing this book. Never give up on your dreams. You are the solution someone else is seeking. You are the answer to many of their questions. You are that shining light at the end of their tunnel. Push. Breathe. Smile. And then say, "thank you."

To my Lord and Savior, Yeshua-Jesus Christ, without You, I am nothing. I love You more with each breath I am given! I surrender all of me to Your service. I trust this book will find its way into the hands of all those You desire to embrace with Your love and grace to help them reach the other side of their pain.

To my amazing husband, Buzz. You have been my rock, standing beside me through it all with an unwavering love and devotion. You offered more support than I ever realized. Thank you for pushing and encouraging me. I love you more than you can possibly imagine!

To Cindy, you have become the sister I never had. Your passion for Jesus has sparked a flame in so many hearts, including my own. Without your constant motivation, even through your own pain, the courage to seek my desires would have likely taken a different path. Your love, friendship, and dedication will always be my inspiration to seek that next step toward following my dreams. Saying 'thank you' is so unfit to measure my gratitude, but it comes from deep inside my heart to yours. I love you, sweet friend!

To Rita, thank you for being an extra set of eyes in the midst of your busy schedule! You are a voice of encouragement, and another sister in my heart. I love and appreciate you!

To Brenda, you deserve an award for going behind my 'deep south' grammar and editing my thoughts within this book! Thank you! Your patience, enthusiasm, love, and joy are commendable traits. You've become a dear friend. Love ya, bless ya!

To my beautiful friends and family, who have provided an overwhelming source of love, prayers, tissues, and a few swift kicks – may our Father richly bless you! Honestly, I am a better person because of your sincerity and caring. I deeply love each of you!

And finally, this book would not be possible without Steve Spillman and True Potential Media. Your passion to get God's goodness into the hands of His people is amazing. Thank you for your guidance and encouragement to make my dream a reality. I've carried this book inside of me for too long. With your wisdom and expertise, I was able to grasp the possibility of putting hope onto paper and running with it. Thank you for bringing out the confidence I had somehow hidden away.

CONTENTS

FOREWORD

Life offers many choices. Each choice has a consequence. At times we regret the choices made because of the consequences attached to them. You will discover each consequence provides an opportunity to accept the consequence, turn things around, or fall into the pit of self-pity. The pit is not a good place to be as it can never provide you with a solution to your pain.

The pit is where I found myself plunging downward. The speed of my drop was increasing, the daylight was growing dim. That was the moment I knew I needed to reach outside of myself and find a rope to cling to.

Self-realization of the daylight slipping away was the first step for me. The defining factor throughout each season was forgiveness.

This book contains hope for the hurting. It is a labor of love for anyone who feels their hope has diminished. Slowly read the words contained within the pages and feel the peace and love I send to you. Again, I remind you, there is always hope! Never give up. Never let go of the rope of hope. Do not only hold onto that rope, but do it with passion and tenacity!

May I also remind you that you are not who others have said you are - you are who YOU say you are. Ask yourself which illegitimate titles have been placed on you and remove them from your vocabulary. Only when you change those words, and crawl out of that pit, will you begin to see who you truly are!

Beauty, peace, and joy lie on the other side of your pain!

INTRODUCTION

If you are reading this book, then my guess would be you have experienced pain in your past, and most likely, you are still dealing with that pain. It may be heartache, anger, or doubt that daily shows up on the doorstep of your thoughts. There are ways to deal with those issues, regardless of which emotion shows up uninvited!

I'm not a doctor, nor do I hold a degree in counseling, but the plaque on my wall reads: "EXPERIENCE." This position is from where I will share my journey with you.

In search for answers to insane issues going on in my life, I made an amazing discovery. Although I felt alone, I was not the first person to experience the same issues. Neither was I the first person to gain victory! For me, the problems I dealt with seemed so profound. And yet for others, my situation may appear to be simple compared to theirs. It appears one's position is most determined by one's perspective.

Many times throughout this book, I will present situations in my life in a very transparent manner. There will be a number of things I will share in hopes of helping you become victorious. Your destiny awaits you - the best is yet to come! This is an exciting time for both you and me; hope is in the air!

I now realize I'm so much stronger than I ever thought myself to be. It is from within this strength I want to reach out to others in need of hope. Honestly, you, too, are much stronger than you've ever perceived yourself to be. Not only are you stronger, you are smarter than you've ever allowed yourself to imagine. Did you catch that? You must allow yourself to become **who you were created to be.**

When I reflect on what I have experienced, some of what I envisioned would kill me has, instead, sharpened me. I discovered an inner strength I would not have found had I not been through these experiences. Some things I felt were devastating served only to take me higher. I now possess a deeper level of understanding of this circle of life. I'm continuously elevating my understanding of who I am and what I am made of. So can you!

My desire for you is that somewhere within this book lies the solution to your healing - true release from the pain you are living with. Or at least, you will find a starting place. We seldom know what others may be suffering internally. We can so often get absorbed in our own problems that we easily forget those around us.

However, I have not forgotten you. You are the reason for this book. You are important. Not only to me but to countless others who will take the journey through these pages.

In the midst of any storm there is always hope. Although you may not be able to see it, there is hope for you regardless of what you may be suffering! A simple ray of hope can change a life!

One thing I want you to remember as you read this book—as long as you keep a glimmer of hope in your heart, you will get through your situation. It may involve some pushing, but it is entirely possible. Let's work together to get you beyond your current situation. People need what you've got. Let's do this!

There is a brand new life experience waiting for you on the other side of your pain!

1. BEYOND BETRAYAL

Personally, I feel being betrayed by someone you love and care about has got to be one of the deepest pains one can endure. My heart experienced betrayal time and time again, yet I still kept going. I kept pretending it eventually would be okay and in time my wounded heart would heal. So far it hasn't healed completely, but thankfully I am almost there. I've gone beyond just surviving to truly thriving. I am now comfortably able to allow a smile on my face through it all.

"Tears of a Clown," some would have said. Often times they were. Smokey Robinson[1] penned that song so many years ago. The older I get, the better I understand about what he was singing.

When my mom passed away in 2012, I wasn't sure I could handle being without her. She was always a symbol of strength that I loved and deeply admired.

---

1   William "Smokey" Robinson, Jr. (February 19, 1940) www.smokeyrobinson.com

We seldom talked, we seldom spent quality time together, heck, rarely did we share affection between the two of us. Yet she was the one with whom I would seek counsel when something I was dealing with needed solving.

Her words sprinkled with criticism seemed to wound me practically every time, but I kept going back. She was my mom, full of wisdom and always willing to give me her two cents worth!

Never though did I give up hope that she would one day open her heart to me. She never did.

I silently remained in my pain. She took hers to her grave.

Life was difficult growing up. Oh, we always had what we needed. And honestly, most of the time we had what we wanted - materialistic things anyway. Yet I always had a love hunger that I could not seem to fill no matter how hard I tried. I looked for fulfillment, but the void always remained.

I'm not proud of some of the things I did years ago. Some of them I would rather have forgotten, but no matter how hard I tried, they lingered in the back of my mind always condemning and causing pain.

Much of what I had been forced to deal with was

> Much of what I had been forced to deal with was nothing more than the consequences of my choices.

nothing more than the consequences of my choices. This became extremely obvious when I stepped back and looked at the problems. This is a hard fact of life. Therefore, we should always think twice before we take action! Some decisions could demand a third look. This is where wise counsel comes in.

Three years after my mother passed away, I feel I discovered why she held me at a distance my entire life. So many questions that had been swirling inside my head for over half a century were finally getting answered. But with each answer came another question because of this new reality.

The merry-go-round was gaining speed. It was going so fast there was no opportunity to jump off. "Please slow down," I cried. Please let me find a place to sit and rest. Please let the world catch up with the force of this ride called life.

I spent too many hours seeking answers. I spoke with family and friends whom I felt I could trust.

I opened my heart to a degree of vulnerability I was neither familiar, nor comfortable with.

Who could help me? What would I further discover? When would the crying stop? Where was I going to get the truth? Why wasn't the truth ever shared with me? There were a million who, what, when, where, and why incidents that produced questions.

Would anything in my life ever again make sense? No! How could it make sense? It was like a nightmare I could not awaken from!

However, inside this head of ours is a phenomenal brain. It houses our mind, both conscious and subconscious. We will talk about them both at some point. Our mind is constantly being programmed from the time we are born. It consumes everything it ever hears spoken and anything seen through our eyes. Eventually we have to take control of what is allowed to be downloaded into our conscious mind because chances are likely they will land in our subconscious mind.

At what do we gaze; what holds our attention?

What and who are we watching on a daily basis?

What and who do we listen to?

What lies have been spoken to us about ourselves that we have chosen to believe? Even deeper than that, what lies are WE speaking to ourselves that we believe?

The inner chatter can do so much harm. Never forget your subconscious mind is always listening to the words you speak, therefore always speak kindness to yourself because yourself is always listening and believing. I will remind you of this throughout this book.

Albert Einstein[2] was quoted as saying, "We cannot solve our problems with the same thinking we used when we created them." Somewhere along the way we must get real with ourselves. We have become masters at putting on a pretty smile and pretending life is something other than what it truly is. Ponder this for a moment: When we look through a mask, reality becomes masked. We do not see reality and it does not see us. Facing the truth

---

2   Albert Einstein – (1879-1955) See www.wikiquotes. org/alberteinstein

brings freedom! We may go through episodes of betrayal caused by others our entire lives, but never allow self-betrayal to happen.

So many times in my life I have felt like running away from home. Running from the pain and leaving behind the familiar to provide myself with a moment of peace. Little did I realize that the pain and familiar surroundings were so embedded

> We simply cannot benefit by running away from those things in our lives that we need to deal with.

within myself they would have followed me wherever I had chosen to hide. We simply cannot benefit by running away from those things in our lives that we need to deal with. Each situation will always offer us an opportunity to grow. Eventually we will begin to realize growth provides us with great abilities to achieve our goals. Happiness is not an impossible dream; it is a state of being from which we can create as much happiness as we desire.

Recently I had an opportunity to lash out at a family member who made a very hurtful statement to me. It was a comment that came from their level of understanding concerning a situation I had experienced. The comment initially seemed to be very negative and self-centered, but once I stepped back and viewed what was said, I honestly had to re-evaluate the entire conversation. I was thrilled when I realized I had no ill feelings toward them. It became clear there was no possible way

I could ever make that family member understand my involvement in the situation, so I let it go! There was so much freedom in being able to do that. The second of anger dissolved almost as quickly as it appeared! I walked away from our conversation with a sense of total peace. That was so much more refreshing than the anger would have ever been. The greatest thing about it was it didn't linger in my mind. I didn't play it back over and over again. I'll trade pain for peace anytime!

Your heart is longing for a much needed time of rest. Your mind is able to provide it. So often we get that order backwards by trying to mend the heart without changing our mind. We can always put a temporary bandage on our heart, but only by correcting our thought life will we mend the wound.

We have taken the first step toward healing. Now, let's get started on this journey to the other side of your pain!

Reflection

Have you ever been hurt or betrayed by someone close to you?

Suggestion

Don't run away from the hurt; face it, and then let it go. Learn to reframe potentially hurtful interactions with others, understanding you have already let go of the past.

Notes: _____

_____

_____

_____

_____

_____

_____

_____

_____

_____

_____

_____

_____

_____

_____

_____

_____

_____

_____

_____
_____
_____
_____
_____
_____
_____
_____
_____
_____
_____
_____
_____
_____
_____
_____
_____
_____
_____
_____
_____
_____
_____
_____
_____
_____
_____
_____

2. WALK WITH ME

During this transition time I have allowed myself to rest and also ponder a lot about the things I have encountered, especially over the past several years. There have been some amazing discoveries yet there have been some incredible moments of pain as well.

Please, allow me to share a little of my journey with you now.

From the time I was a little girl, I had always felt out of place. A little bit different than the rest of my family. There were so many occasions at family gatherings where I felt I was the odd ball.

Then there were times I would wonder why I did not look like my little brother. Was there a reason why our hair and eyes were a different color? I would even catch myself questioning why our skin tones were different. He would easily sunburn and I would quickly tan! Yet more often than not those thoughts would be shoved into the back corner of my mind to be left alone for the time being. Maybe it was normal. After all, we weren't the only siblings I knew who didn't particularly favor each other.

> From childhood, the root of rejection was deeply embedded into our very souls.

My maternal grandmother treated me very badly when I was a child. Sadly, she also mistreated my cousin, Theresa. She and I both grew up dealing with the pain of being handled as an outcast within our own family. From childhood, the root of rejection was deeply embedded into our very souls.

One particular year we had a family Christmas party. My grandmother had a spectacular tree in the living room with blinking lights, ornaments, and tinsel. Underneath the tree, the floor was covered with beautifully wrapped presents. When the time came to open those gifts, of course, we children were thrilled to begin!

We waited in anticipation as my grandmother looked intently around the room. Suddenly she called on Theresa and me to hand out the presents to everyone there. We were so excited and felt privileged to have been chosen for such a task. As the laughter and shouts filled the room, we hurriedly passed out the gifts!

As the pile of presents dwindled down, there was confusion in my mind as we handed out the last gift from under the tree. Was there not a gift for Theresa and myself? Patiently, she and I waited for our grandmother to hopefully hand us a gift; surely we did a good job and made everyone happy.

As we waited it became obvious that there was nothing wrapped in pretty paper for us. The pain from that memory in both of our six-year-old hearts lasted for many years.

To make matters worse, when I was 19 years old, she called our home one afternoon to cause more heartache. It had been many years since we had seen or spoken with her. When I answered the phone, she asked if I was my mother. I replied no and asked if I could help her. She then wanted to know with whom she was speaking. I politely asked with whom did she want to speak?

She called my name, I replied yes, and she proceeded to tell me who she was. I spoke, although I was a bit surprised to hear her voice after so many years.

After the awkward moment filled with simple talk, she asked me an earth-shattering question...

"Has your mother ever told you that you do not belong to your dad?"

I was stunned for a moment in time! I told her I did not believe a word of what she was saying and exclaimed that even if he wasn't my biological father, he would forever be my daddy!

I then hung up.

Much to my shock and bewilderment, I held myself together and called my mom at work asking her to please come home. We had a long discussion about the episode and it was agreed that my grandmother was only trying to create more conflict as she had always done in the past.

The conversation then became taboo within the family.

Eventually it faded away… or so I thought.

You see, in the back of my mind I wondered about a few of the things mentioned during our talk. There were times when I tried to figure out why my grandmother would do something so unkind and hurtful. I never got solid answers to my many questions, but I let it go as best I could.

To make this long story short, I later discovered through the means of a DNA test that the man who I knew as daddy my entire life, was indeed not my biological father.

My grueling search began.

I won't go into detail of all the things I experienced over the course of three years, but I will say it was extremely difficult. In a matter of a single sentence, it felt as though I had lost half of the family I had known for over 50 years. All of a sudden the ones with whom I shared my childhood were no longer related to the other half of me – the other half of me who I didn't even know! She was there but she had no identity. She existed but she was half of a person. Just who was the other half of me?

The million questions I previously had were basically answered yet another million questions arose.

Now before you say my discovery should not have

changed anything with the family I had always known, I must with sadness tell you it did. The most important person was the man who I so lovingly called daddy. He had an extremely difficult time accepting the fact that he had never been told the truth from my mom. He chose to take the path of anger and became self-absorbed. He was mostly concerned with thoughts of how he must look like a fool to everyone else who knew the truth.

> It was at this time in my life I needed daddy to wrap his arms around me ...

It was at this time in my life I needed daddy to wrap his arms around me and tell me it didn't matter; that I would always and forever be his daughter. He never did. He could no longer look at me the same. His anger toward my mom turned quickly into hatred and became pain for both him and me. He chose to close the door between us, blaming me for uncovering the truth.

Honestly, he never even asked if I was okay. Several years passed without a word spoken between us. The pain within my heart has healed. I still miss him dearly, but I can't change his heart. I wish him well. I pray that one day he understands just how much I still love and miss him.

My daughter, my only child, refuses to talk about the entire situation. Neither do I have the freedom to share any of my continuing journeys with her. She has no interest in participating in or knowing any details of my discoveries. I'm certain in her heart she has her reasons.

I hold onto hope that one day she will want to know. Odd how my heart always longed for my mom to share her heart with me, yet it appears my daughter doesn't want to know anything about mine. Heartache - yes. Healing – yes! On the other side of my pain is… I am still joyfully filling in the blanks!

The search for my paternal family was a difficult journey, but after three long years full of searching and seeking, I found my family. Actually, they found me!

Now, at this point you would again think that everything worked out and life is grand, correct? That was the hope of my heart anyway.

> For many nights I would lie in bed thinking how it would feel when I finally discovered my paternal family.

For many nights I would lie in bed thinking how it would feel when I finally discovered my paternal family. My deepest desire was to look into someone's eyes and see the other half of me. What would we say to each other? Did we favor? Did I have more half-siblings? Would they be accepting of me, or worse yet, would they even want to meet me?

May I tell you I have gained three half-brothers? Yay!!

During this time, some new relatives have embraced me – some have shunned me. Some have treated me as if they have loved me my whole life – others have turned their backs and walked away. I'm sad for them, not for myself.

There has been so much growth in these past several years and I am grateful for the experience. It has made a stronger and better version of me. A new me. A different me. A fulfilled me. A me who I'm still discovering, yet, a me that I have always been, and somehow always known. It seemed for years I knew there was something missing in my heart but my brain simply could not process the information my heart was trying to share.

Puzzle pieces finally fitting into place.

Even today, I feel my search is still taking me places. I feel there are more relatives who have felt I was out there, too. There has actually been a deep bonding with one of my half-siblings, and he too has felt he wasn't alone! I thought that was amazing, to say the least. He and I have a lot of catching up to do!

Facing those things that are bothering you will be the first step to take on your journey of finding hope and healing. Learning to separate the pain and not allowing it to become your identity will turn things around for you. I'm not in any way saying your pain isn't real, I know it is, but it doesn't have to be who you are. The pain is not your true self. It is not who you are deep down inside. That person is anxiously waiting for the day you discover them; that special day when you relate to the truth.

I have a quote by a fictitious character on my wall which reads, "There are moments which mark your life. Moments when you realize nothing will ever be the same and time is divided into two parts, before this and after this…" Change is inevitable; our attitude about change is a choice.

So, what about my hopes? Well, one of them you are holding in your hands. This book is designed to be a source of hope for you. There will never be a time when you are alone and without someone who can relate to your pain. I may not have had the same experience as you have had, but my heart knows rejection, abandonment, betrayal, and pain. But you must know my heart has also found love, peace, and joy! This is also possible for you!

Again I want to express, "you are so much stronger than you have ever perceived yourself to be." There is an untapped source of strength deep within you and it is waiting for you to dig in and find it. You have the innate ability. You have the intelligence. You have the tenacity to hang on no matter what.

As Henry Ford is quoted as saying, "Whether you think you can or whether you think you can't, you are correct."[3] It's all in your perception of yourself. Reminder question… Do you know that every time you speak to yourself, you are listening and you hear every word? Therefore, learn to speak words of encouragement to yourself. Be kind and forgiving, always extending grace. Express words of gratitude to yourself for the good things you have done. Once you learn to pay attention to what you are thinking about, you will be able to make a huge shift in your perception. This will bring about tremendous change in your current and future self.

---

3   Henry Ford - (1863-1947) www.quotespedia.com

When you find yourself hurting, allow yourself to do so, observe it but only for a short while - then move on. Change your focus. Look at the many things that are good in your life and concentrate on any one of those. When your heart song is replaced with gratitude, the pain has to leave; it may visit occasionally but it will soon get the message that it is not welcomed.

Reflection

Are you willing to face and confront those things that are bothering or holding you back?

Suggestion

You truly are able to separate the pain from your true, authentic self and refuse to wear it like a back-pack. The pain you are experiencing is not your identity. Your first step is often reminding yourself of who you truly are.

Notes: _____

_____
_____
_____
_____
_____
_____
_____
_____
_____
_____
_____
_____
_____
_____
_____
_____
_____
_____

Walk With Me

_____
_____
_____
_____
_____
_____
_____
_____
_____
_____
_____
_____
_____
_____
_____
_____
_____
_____
_____
_____
_____
_____
_____
_____
_____
_____

3. YOUR INNER WARRIOR

Inside of you is where you must search for the warrior. All of your healing is there. Now it's time to concentrate on how to connect with that warrior. You see, once you begin to see yourself as you truly are, all else will slowly begin to diminish. Your identity is not who anyone has told you that you are. No one has the right to define you except the true you. Only you can change the existing definition of yourself if you are not pleased with your current reality.

Each and every thought you give your attention to will form the person whom you will become. Where you are today is a direct result of the thoughts you've had in your past. Pause just a moment and think about this comment, "Pay attention." What has your attention cost you? Time, maybe? Focus, maybe? Or even creating the very thing you did not want yet chose to pay attention to! If you must ever pay attention, make certain it is worth the cost.

I can remember many years ago, having a very difficult time finding anything good or acceptable about myself. There were so many negative thoughts going through my mind and at times some of them would come out of my mouth! Big mistake!

I never extended grace toward myself. It seemed I fell short at most everything I did. I was unhappy with myself and that caused me to be unhappy with life.

More often than not there were harsh words being spoken and sadly, the majority of those words were coming from within me! I would call myself names. I would see myself as a failure, a mistake. This would lead to intense pain and then my mind would stay focused on those negative thoughts throughout the day. I would feel depressed, as if my life was useless and wasted. Never did I realize the things I stayed focused on were the very things that were causing me harm and producing the effects of my own thoughts. They were shaping the reality of my life. If you have found yourself to be caught in this vicious cycle, it's time to put on the brakes.

When any thought is given attention, it expands.

One very important truth I hope you grab hold of is this – when any thought is given attention, it expands. Good or bad. If you focus on that thought, and your emotions become attached to the thought, it slips into your heart. Once it becomes a heart issue, it then enters your subconscious mind and goes into autopilot, becoming a part of who you are.

Your subconscious mind begins to shape you according to the thought. This is part of the process of developing your identity. Everything begins with a thought.

Our silent, subconscious thoughts become the language in which we speak to another person's heart. In other words, what we think about ourselves is what we speak to them. Not verbally, but by the thoughts we have constantly entertained about ourselves. Those silent thoughts are communicated to others in their heart and are picked up by their subconscious mind. Personally, I have called myself some names in the past that I would never want someone else to feel I am! Yet when I say these things to myself enough times I begin to believe them, then they enter my subconscious mind and become who I created myself to be. Those thoughts then become my identity.

Have you ever met someone and instantly felt uncomfortable? Maybe you felt they weren't being honest. Maybe you even went as far as questioning their motives. This is due to the person they believe they are in their heart but not being that person who they are portraying to be when you meet. We may not understand why we feel a particular way about someone, but our feelings are formed by what our subconscious mind heard in silence.

You see, our thoughts precede us, therefore, those first unconsciously projected thoughts we have been focused on is actually how we introduce ourselves to people, or even animals for that matter. The language of the heart received from our subconscious mind can be heard even by the physically deaf. It is spoken with every heartbeat.

I've learned that our initial introduction is very difficult to change until our subconscious language begins to change our heart. This process first begins by changing our thoughts. This is one reason that first impressions generally remain for a while. The heart and the subconscious mind are so interconnected.

So, regardless of the Sunday morning suits and the plastic smiles some hide behind, they're truly not hiding at all. The hearts of other people hear us, the real us. They hear the real person whom we are constantly, subconsciously projecting onto their hearts; even without spoken words. Thoughts are quicker than words and when emotions are attached to thoughts they become even more powerful.

"As a man thinks in his heart, so is he."

The Bible even references this in the book of Proverbs, chapter 23 verse 7 says, "As a man thinks in his heart, so is he." So, not only do we become what we think about, what we think about is who we become. This is who we are to others! Let's teach our heart the language of love and it will then teach our subconscious mind!

Now, it looks as though we may need to work on changing our thoughts, doesn't it? We want to become the fullness of who we are. Not remain the person who has been created by the actions of others or our negative self image. One of the fastest ways to recognize an unwanted thought is to place a couple of notes around your location with a big question mark on them. Every time you see the note ask yourself, "What am I thinking about at this moment?" Pause and think back for a few seconds and you will see where your thoughts have been going, you will remember the inner chatter that talks too much throughout the day! Negative self talk can be so harmful.

When we learn how to recognize and thus stop a destructive thought process from completing its course, we can turn them around onto another path – one of encouragement and love. With practice we will become more aware of our thoughts thus allowing us to extend our boundaries. This will lead to a life with no limitations. You truly can become the person you have always dreamed you were but never had the courage to create!

When we can finally lasso thoughts by becoming aware of them, we can download the proper thoughts. That will help us make a difference in the way we see ourselves. This is so exciting and brings so much happiness. Remember also to smile and speak a few good words to yourself about your accomplishment at that moment. "Yourself" will reciprocate with feelings of joy! This joy will produce hope. Hope will produce balance and ultimately victory! You are getting closer to the other side of your pain!

Reflection

Are you willing to begin the process of changing or redirecting your thoughts?

Suggestion

Make a concentrated effort to capture those negative thoughts and replace them with words that will uplift and encourage the new you who is being formed.

Notes: _____

_____

_____

_____

_____

_____

_____

_____

_____

_____

_____

_____

_____

_____

_____

_____

_____

_____

_____

_____

Your Inner Warrior

4. THE REMOTE CONTROL SYSTEM

For most of my life I was a cigarette smoker. I started smoking because I was dared and ridiculed by friends because I didn't want to join them for a cigarette. I grew up in a family of smokers so it became a natural habit to pick up. Since most everyone in my family smoked, I really didn't see any problems with it. My parents were never in favor of my smoking habit and let's just say... I was firmly disciplined!

About the same time I began smoking, I developed asthma. Once my lungs began to give out on me as an adult, I knew I could not continue with the habit I had formed so many years before. I feared I had waited too long to put down the cigarettes, but neither could I imagine my life without them. Yet, deep inside I knew I simply had to quit smoking. I had twin grandchildren on the way. I wanted to be around to watch them grow up. I wanted to make memories. This gave me the desire to live more than I wanted another cigarette!

The day I visited my lung doctor, he had nothing but bad news to share...

The day I visited my lung doctor, he had nothing but bad news to share with me from the results of my tests. I took a deep breath and left his office. As I was walking to my car, a tsunami of emotions hit me right in the gut. Along with the emotions came questions. Up and down, back and forth, every which way I could think did not offer one sense of peace. I was a wreck. A crying, messed up wreck.

I will spare you the final moments I had with the last cigarette I smoked, but I shared it with a cup of coffee, angry tears, and an incredibly strong desire to defeat the addiction. You see, there had been so many times in my past where I tried to stop smoking, only to fail within a very short time. I'd pick right back up where I left off.

Not one time after those failed attempts did I pat myself on the back and say, "Good job for trying to quit smoking." Instead, I would feel like a failure, beat up on myself, and go grab a cigarette as though it could offer some sympathy!

My angry tears flowed because I had no one to blame but myself. How could I have brought about such a mess? I had refused to listen for so many years to so many people who begged me to quit smoking! I'd politely listen as they rattled on about the dangers, then smile and walk away. It would anger me when they insisted I put them down, but it angered me now, since I refused to listen.

Honestly, I was the source of my own anger. I surely couldn't take the blame, right? That's human nature, blaming others. It began with Adam in the Garden blaming Eve for taking the first bite when approached by God, "It was that woman you gave me!" (Genesis 3:12)

So, the good news is I did quit smoking. That very same day. My love affair with nicotine ended and I am so grateful it is far behind me.

Now, you may be wondering why I shared this story. Well, glad you asked! There is a purpose for my story. I discovered a valuable lesson during this season of kicking the smoking habit. A lesson I want to share with you.

A friend of mine and I were talking not long ago. She told me that she was trying her best to quit smoking. She stated she desperately wants to quit the habit this time. I was thrilled for her, but neither had I condemned her for her past struggles. During our conversation, I told her about the remote control system I had to apply when I finally put down cigarettes.

She laughed and asked, "What do you mean the Remote Control System?"

I explained, "For about six months after I had quit, it seemed that everywhere I went there were people smoking. For instance, I would pull up to a traffic light and the person beside me would be smoking. Or riding down the highway, minding my own business, someone would pass me with a cigarette in their mouth. I could even be walking across the parking lot of our local store and I would walk past someone standing outside smoking! It seemed the cigarettes had a life of their own and inevitably they followed me wherever I would go!"

She exclaimed with a chuckle, "I know the feeling! I, too, have noticed that happening and every time it makes me want to smoke right along with them!"

That's when I explained to her my discovery of the Remote Control System!

"It's actually easier than you think," I said. "The next time you notice someone who seems to be enjoying a cigarette, rather than staring at them and thinking about how much you would like to have one too, simply look away. You are holding the remote control of your mind and you can change your thoughts as quickly as turning away and looking at something else. Your remote control will change the channel if you use it."

"Wow!" she exclaimed, "Is it really that easy?"

"Yes, it's that easy!"

> Understand that YOU hold the remote control to your mind.

Understand that YOU hold the remote control to your mind. YOU have the power to flip the channel any moment of any day; this stirs up a strength inside of you that is hard to put into words. It's amazing when you realize you are in control rather than your mind taking over the situation!

I was once told by a pastor that what we behold we become. I've never forgotten that. If you don't want to be a smoker, don't stare at anyone smoking! Never pay attention to temptation; it simply costs too much! Making the commitment is like putting new batteries in your remote control. Remember: The Remote Control will not work if you don't use it!

Use the remote control that you possess. Change the channel. Put the right direction in your thoughts and this will bring about a positive change in your life.

When we can reach a point where we think about what we are thinking about, we have reached a new level of awareness. As a child, most of us are never truly trained to be aware of our thoughts or how to control the events in our imagination. Allowing the mind to aimlessly wander is not productive and will always stunt your growth. It can rob you of your dreams and steal your hope if you allow your thoughts to run free and unrestrained.

Reflection

By now you are getting an understanding of the power your thoughts carry. Are you willing to take control of your thought life and refuse to allow thoughts to control you?

Suggestion

Identify and replace the thoughts that interfere with gaining victory over the pain you carry. Let's work on it becoming "the" pain rather than "your" pain! You are not identified by any pain!

Notes: _____

_____

_____

_____

_____

_____

_____

_____

_____

_____

_____

_____

_____

_____

_____

_____

_____

_____

_____
_____
_____
_____
_____
_____
_____
_____
_____
_____
_____
_____
_____
_____
_____
_____
_____
_____
_____
_____
_____
_____
_____
_____
_____
_____
_____
_____
_____
_____

5. The Power of Suggestion

Have you heard the story of the woman who went to work one morning feeling relaxed and restful after a fun weekend? We will call her Sue. When Sue got to her desk, the lady sitting beside her asked how she was feeling. Sue exclaimed with a smile it had been a nice and relaxing weekend.

The co-worker proceeds to tell her she looks as if she didn't get enough rest. She then wants to know if Sue was feeling okay. Much to Sue's surprise, she explains to the co-worker that she was fine and did indeed get enough rest.

After Sue has been busily working on her project, she decides she wants to grab a cup of coffee so she heads around the corner to the break room. Feeling chipper, she smiled as she smelled the coffee. When she arrived in the break room, she is met by another co-worker. The co-worker looked intently at her for a moment. Sue asked her if there was something wrong. "I'm not sure," replied the co-worker, "it's just you look a little pale this morning. Are you feeling well?"

Sue stopped for a moment, analyzed how she was feeling and began to wonder if maybe something could be wrong that she had not yet noticed. Silently she scans her thoughts and puts her focus on the words these two co-workers had spoken to her.

She managed to brush it off, poured her coffee and headed back to her desk. As she walked down the hall, she overheard a conversation about a lady who had come down with the flu. She turns toward the ladies who are talking and asks what the lady's symptoms were.

The same two ladies began to tell her the things the lady had experienced, one of them being pale, and the other symptom, looking like she was tired. Sue listened as they talked but she didn't hear what else they said. She missed the part about the lady living in another state. She could hear only the words ringing through her mind that maybe she had the flu and didn't even know it! After all, she had been told that morning that she looked a little tired and also seemed to appear pale.

By lunchtime, Sue felt very ill.

By lunchtime, Sue felt very ill. She left work early and went to the doctor to be tested for the flu. The doctor explained to her there was no flu outbreak in her hometown; flu season had not arrived. She tested negative. Sue is a classic example of the power of suggestion. She clearly allowed her thoughts to convince herself she was sick.

Had Sue used her remote control and taken control of her thoughts, she would not have gone through that episode. It's time we understand how our thoughts influence every aspect of our lives.

I want to share another brief story with you which was once told to me. I can't give credit to the originator because I do not know who it was. This story is an amazing way to see the power of our thoughts and help us understand our mind. The story begins with two monks walking down a dirt road on their way to their afternoon pilgrimage. They come upon a young girl standing on the side of the road. She was dressed in a long, beautifully flowing gown. In the middle of the road was a mud puddle. As she was trying to figure out how to cross the mud to get to the other side of the road, one of the monks picked her up, walked through the mud and put her down on the other side.

He crossed back over to where the second monk was and they continued their journey in silence. These two monks walked for almost five hours before they reached their destination. As they were coming up to the front of the location, the second monk turned to the first monk and said, "You know, you really should not have done what you did. We monks are not even supposed to touch a woman, so you really shouldn't have done that."

So the first monk looks at him and says, "Oh, are you still carrying that girl? I put her down hours ago."

So, the second monk was carrying that girl around in his head for almost five hours. The event was still in his mind and he was walking with that burden in his thoughts. This reveals the reluctance of our mind to let go of the past and live in the present.

Once you learn to use your remote control to change the channel in your mind, you will get closer to the path that leads to the other side of your pain.

Reflection

Are you beginning to see how thoughts can easily consume you?

Suggestion

Learn to think about what you are thinking about. Take time to redirect those thoughts that produce feelings of pain. Re-train your focus to think on the things that bring you peace, happiness and freedom!

Notes: _____

_____

_____

_____

_____

_____

_____

_____

_____

_____

_____

_____

_____

_____

_____

_____

_____

_____

_____

_____

_____

_____
_____
_____
_____
_____
_____
_____
_____
_____
_____
_____
_____
_____
_____
_____
_____
_____
_____
_____
_____
_____
_____
_____
_____
_____
_____
_____
_____
_____
_____

6. HELD CAPTIVE

We are so often held captive by our thoughts. We so easily say the sky is the limit but what if we shoot for the stars? What if the moon is farther than the sky or deeper than the stars? What if there are no boundaries beyond the stars? What if the only boundaries that exist are the ones we set for ourselves?

Unless we are willing to grow beyond our preconceived limits, we are destined to remain tied down to the same old patterns and mindsets. We will wind up not going farther than we have already been. Listen to that again - we will never go farther than the limitations of our mind! How boring would that be?

Move the boundaries that have been placed on you by yourself or others. Break the chains that have held you captive for so long. You truly are without limits once you are freed from those boundaries!

One afternoon, while driving home, I fell in behind a vehicle on the road to our community. I did not recognize the automobile, but I caught myself very intently looking at it. I began wondering how it had gotten in the bad condition that it appeared to be in. The back window had been busted out and they had duct taped a piece of polyurethane onto the opening where the window should have been. It was very loud as if the muffler may have had a hole in it. That was my guess anyway.

The vehicle was dented and rusted in many places and had a few spots where someone had taken spray paint and decorated it with brightly colored swirls! It was in desperate need of being washed. The vehicle also needed mechanical work to stop the smoke that was coming from the tailpipe.

Backing away from the exhaust a short distance, I began to reflect on the possibilities of why they may have allowed the vehicle to get in that condition. As we rounded the curve, the driver extended his arm to motion to me he was going to turn into the next driveway. I knew the family who lived at that location. As I slowed down, I realized who this man was. I caught his reflection in the side view mirror. I knew his dad. And although I had not yet met him, the genes were strong and he could not deny who his father was!

Once he turned into his dad's driveway, I began to think about that family. I viewed the lifestyle they had chosen to live; it had been passed down several generations. They, too, repeatedly adopted the same lifestyle of poverty as their ancestors had chosen. I wondered if any of them had ever been told they didn't have to live in poverty. And if they had been told, what would it take for any of them to believe they could live differently since they each showed no signs of changing directions? Every one of their individual lives mirrored each other's. They were bound up by the beliefs they had accepted. These beliefs created mindsets and the mindsets created the limits in their lives. I find this situation such a sad reality for so many.

Reflect with me for a moment here. From as far back as we can remember, we were instructed by someone. Most likely a parent or close relative in our first few years. As a toddler, we basically learned by observance. Next we began school.

> From as far back as we can remember, we were instructed by someone.

We were assigned teachers and those teachers began to pour the subjects into our little minds which had been chosen by the school board. Let's step a little deeper into this thought.

For instance, we had Miss Jones for math in the first grade class; she may have taught us that one apple plus one apple equals two apples. On the other hand, if we had been assigned Mr. Smith, he may have taught us that one pineapple plus one pineapple equals two pineapples. Take away one of the pineapples and you have only one pineapple left. It's the same addition, using different examples, with one equation going a step farther than the other.

Half of Miss Jones' students and half of Mr. Smith's students carry their lessons into the second grade and are assigned Mrs. Williams for math. Mrs. Williams begins her math lessons where Mr. Smith left off. Those students who already knew how to take away one did very well. Those students who had not been taught that same math technique did not do as well.

As children, we continued in school, constantly being taught from an agenda based on the perspective of the teacher. We learned reading, writing, arithmetic, and everything else on the school board's agenda. We were also taught things like social skills which may or may not have been different than what we were taught at home. We were wide open to receive any and everything that was being told to us by total strangers for eight hours a day, nine months out of the year, for twelve long years. Since it is human nature to mimic our surroundings, just how much of our teachers do we carry most of our entire lives?

> All of us, at some point in our lives, have been taught, persuaded, and programmed by someone else.

By now most of us know how college, the military, our workplace, our church, and people with whom we have had contact, have influenced us. All of us, at some point in our lives, have been taught, persuaded, and programmed by someone else.

This became my very first lesson on the power of mindsets. As I began to study and gain a little knowledge of mindsets, and how they affect us, I acquired a great deal of insight. One of the things that stuck out in my mind was a quote by St. Francis Xavier.[4] "Give me the child until he is seven and I will give you the man." It seems St. Francis understood the importance of molding and shaping a child in his first seven years. This is the period when children develop their core beliefs. This is from where they will model the adults in their lives. It is the most critical time in a child's life. What they learn will follow them for the remainder of their lives. That is, until they believe a better way may exist than the way that was presented to them, they will remain in the same mindset.

As adults, they may not understand why they feel the way they do about different events in their lives. It can all be backtracked to their childhood. There's a Bible scripture that says, "Train up a child in the way he should go, and he will not depart from it" (Proverbs 22:6). This fits perfectly with the aforementioned quote from St. Francis Xavier. So if we turn that around I can also see it meaning how we train a child will shape him as an adult. It's obviously worth much thought!

During my study, I also learned we can change our core beliefs if we desire to do so. The first step is discovering the negative and untrue core beliefs! Then we can begin changing the channel in our minds, every time we catch ourselves dwelling on the negative. It is past time to focus on the positive. Negativity comes in so many shapes and sizes! From the downright obvious to the subtle little whispers.

---

4   St. Francis Xavier - (1506-1552) See www.britannica.
com

Another good quote to ponder while on your journey says, "The truth is, unless you let go, unless you forgive yourself, unless you forgive the situation, unless you realize the situation is over, you cannot move forward." Steve Maraboli.[5] He is also noted as saying, "The very thing that is causing you pain is building you up." And to these two quotes, I will add that forgiveness for others plays a crucial part in our recovery!

This is one more reason it is imperative for us to realize we must release the pain. We must also never give up looking for a way to forgive those involved who seem to be unforgivable. Holding onto and dwelling on any pain will only increase it until it finally consumes you. Remember it is said that holding onto anger and unforgiveness is like you drinking poison and expecting the other person to die. It only hurts you in the end.

You are the creator of your own life's reality. Every moment you spend reflecting on the past is a moment of your future you can never recover. Why take that pain into the future with you? Let it remain in the past. Bury it under a pile of forgiveness so you can take your next step to the other side of your pain!

---

5   Steve Maraboli (April 18, 1975) www.stevemaraboli.net

Reflection

Are you ready to leave the pain behind? Are you willing to release it and set yourself free?

Suggestion

Stay focused on where you are going and not where you've been. The present needs you and your future self awaits your arrival. Show up, straighten up and walk proudly!

Notes: _____

_____
_____
_____
_____
_____
_____
_____
_____
_____
_____
_____
_____
_____
_____
_____
_____
_____
_____

_____

_____

_____

_____

_____

_____

_____

_____

_____

_____

_____

_____

_____

_____

_____

_____

_____

_____

_____

_____

_____

_____

_____

_____

_____

_____

_____

7. FINDING YOUR PURPOSE

When I made the decision to write this book, the first thing I scribbled in my notes was my purpose for doing so. I asked myself, "Should I really be writing a book about heartache, pain and ultimately walking in victory"? With an emphatic YES, this is what I scribbled – "I want to write a book because I feel there are others out there who need to draw a sense of strength from my past experiences and lessons learned. I want to impart hope to those who feel hopeless, direction for those who feel lost, and a hug for those who feel unloved. I want to help set them free and inspire them to push through to become who they truly are – the very best version of themselves."

There is a certain comfort in knowing there is someone out there who understands you. Someone who can relate to the depth of pain you may be dealing with. The circumstances do not necessarily have to be the same, but pain has a way of expressing itself so others can relate. Don't misunderstand me, I know firsthand there are what seem to be greater degrees of pain, but regardless of where you are right now, there is a light at the end of the tunnel! If you will hold on and never allow hope to die, you will reach the end of that tunnel called pain!

> I have learned to not pass judgment on someone else's journey.

On the other side of the spectrum, it's best to understand that the Broadway Production which plays in our mind can often times be viewed as an elementary school production by someone else. I have learned to not pass judgment on someone else's journey. As we discussed a little earlier, the degree of pain that I have experienced may seem like a trivial matter to you, but it can have devastating results on me. So, I never expect anyone to truly understand where I am in the midst of my journey. Neither do I expect them to be able to identify with the pain I feel if they have never dealt with what I am going through.

In the beginning I did not realize these things. I left conversations feeling neglected and misunderstood. I would want to run and hide somewhere so I could lick my wounds, as they say, and comfort myself in a bath of self-pity. This resulted in falling right back into the trap of feeling as though I was the only person who has ever been through something as devastating. I would begin thinking someone's perceived lack of sympathy meant a lack of caring toward my problems. There were also times I felt they truly didn't care about me either. This would start that downward spiral into feelings of betrayal and abandonment. That becomes a difficult place to bounce out of until we learn to stop the thoughts before they begin to grow.

When we are hurting, it is so easy to lash out at others because we automatically expect them to 'get it' when we are trying to communicate with them. We fail to realize they can never get as deep into our feelings as we can because they have truly not felt our pain. Once we can learn that valuable lesson, we can experience a sense of peace from just knowing that fact. Sometimes, all someone else can do is just be there to listen. That is often an outlet for us to release pain, but it isn't necessarily always what we thought they may provide. And that's okay. Just let it go and remember, they are doing the best they can from their level of understanding.

We can often get ourselves into a mess if we place expectations on someone who has never experienced what we are dealing with. It's virtually impossible for anyone to fulfill our expectations because they can't feel our personal pain. In our mind we unconsciously create a scene of how we think others should respond. These expectations come from the needs of our wounded heart. This is always a formula for added pain.

Their response to your pain may not be what we thought we needed to hear, but it truly doesn't mean they don't care. They can only respond from their level of understanding of our situation, not from our personal level of experience.

The sooner we learn that others cannot sincerely relate directly to our pain, the less weight we will add to our pain load! Besides, the more we talk about the pain, the longer it will take to subside. So, if our thoughts naturally begin to sharpen by giving attention to them, it's time to change the channel! If we don't want the pain to continue we must re-direct our thoughts. In reality, we are adding to the problem by placing our attention on it. Becoming aware of this propensity helps us to not react to what others may say, do, or neglect.

Try to picture the pain being seeds, thoughts being fertilizer and the words being water. What do you think will grow? Now turn that around and picture the joy you feel knowing you are reaching the other side of your pain. Place your focus on the joy which fertilizes your thoughts and talk about the direction you want your life to go from this point. Now you've made a change! You just used your remote control! Yay!

> There will always be times when your thoughts will visit the things that have brought you pain.

There will always be times when your thoughts will visit the things that have brought you pain. That's okay, too. Just don't allow yourself to linger in those thoughts. Release them and move in another direction. In time you will find this easier to do. There may even be times you need to give yourself permission to cry, just don't hang out there for long enough to get comfortable!

Eventually, you will develop the skill of thinking about what you are thinking about. Being able to pull your thoughts back into the right direction is so refreshing. It is also productive. Immediately, change your mind when you feel you are having thoughts that bring you pain about any situation. And, for the most part, our thoughts are typically worse than the actual problem. They can so easily become super inflated if allowed to overstay their welcome! Remember, changing your mind doesn't allow pain to set up a tent and visit for a while! Your destination is found on the road that leads to the other side of your pain!

Reflection

Do you ever feel as though there is no one who "gets it" when it comes to your situation?

Suggestion

Take a deep breath and accept the fact that you may never find that person; that's okay. Bringing others into your pain can often times increase that pain. Remember, when you focus on the pain it will expand. Instead, focus on your future self to expand healing!

Notes: _____

_____

_____

_____

_____

_____

_____

_____

_____

_____

_____

_____

_____

_____

_____

_____

_____

_____

Finding Your Purpose

_____
_____
_____
_____
_____
_____
_____
_____
_____
_____
_____
_____
_____
_____
_____
_____
_____
_____
_____
_____
_____
_____
_____
_____
_____
_____
_____
_____
_____
_____

8. IT ALL COMES DOWN TO A CHOICE

Let's agree to establish a few things in our healing journey. Ultimately, we will have to make a choice of how we will react to any and all of life's issues. The results we achieve will be determined by these choices, whether they lead to good or bad results. We can own the results or we can continue to make excuses as to "why me." Set your intentions to rise above any limits you have ever conceived for yourself. Go beyond every boundary that has been placed in your life. You are unstoppable! There is nothing you cannot do if you set your mind to doing it.

Today, I want to ask you to begin spending some quality time with yourself. Get to know who you are. Chances are, once you look beyond the exterior and search deep within your heart, you will see the perfection of who God created you to be! You will have to go beyond the thoughts, dive deeper than the discouragement, far away from the self-condemnation, into that quiet place.

It may be a little deeper than you have ever been, but it's worth every moment it takes to find the real you!

> How long would you hang around someone who talked to you the way you talk to yourself?

In addition, I encourage you to work on changing the way you treat yourself. How long would you hang around someone who talked to you the way you talk to yourself? My guess would be: NOT VERY LONG! My challenge to you is to find yourself a mirror and sit down in front of it. Smile at yourself and call your own name – with a kind voice begin to speak these words: "(your name), I love you and I forgive you." Say it again and again until it begins to sink in. Do this daily for 30 days and watch your heart soften and your face begin to shine. It entirely changes your countenance and begins healing your heart.

Again, I remind you that we are always listening to ourselves when we talk to ourselves. Our subconscious mind pays attention to every detail, every word spoken. We should always speak life to ourselves. The Bible tells us, "Death and life are in the power of the tongue, and those who love it shall eat the fruit thereof" (Proverbs 18:21). Words are considered seeds. A seed produces after its own kind. Plant an apple seed and you will get an apple tree, etc. Words of life will produce life. Words of death produce death. We hold the Power of Life & Death in Our Tongues… Blessing or Cursing. Today, make the choice of Blessing!

It's time to change the way you see yourself as well as the way you treat yourself. Let go of the past and begin to live in the future—the future you were created for and designed to possess. It is very important to not allow the storms that are raging around you to become storms on the inside of you. There can always, always, be peace within. Once things begin to change on the inside, they will also change on the outside. As William Arthur Ward is quoted as saying, "Happiness is an inside job."[6] This girl wholeheartedly agrees!

Take time to determine what you are saying to yourself. You must change your inner dialogue. If you are constantly getting the same results over and over again, then you must find the boundary you have set in that area of your life. This is where the subconscious mind has to be reprogrammed because it is running on autopilot and producing your beliefs, not your wants. It will always sabotage you until it is corrected and accepts your new boundaries. Once you determine those boundaries, you can then begin to change the subconscious mind to agree with the changes you want to permanently make in your life.

Would you like to really confuse your subconscious mind? Try bathing with the opposite hand you normally use! Talk about an experience! You will notice you immediately feel uncomfortable doing something differently that your subconscious mind has set in stone. Has it hit you that you never have to think about what to do when you shower? You have a routine, and it takes no concentration to follow through with it on a daily basis.

6   William Arthur Ward (12/17/1921-3/30/1994) www. williamauthurward.com

Here is another fun thing to do: Try brushing your teeth with the opposite hand. You will have to think about every step to take in order to accomplish that simple task, whereas if you don't change things up, you will fly right through the process hardly ever having to think about it. This is the power of our subconscious mind!

Have you ever arrived somewhere and thought to yourself, "How did I get here"? One minute you're pulling out of your driveway and the next you are pulling into a parking spot. There may be an entire highway you don't recall coming down. This is an example of your subconscious mind running on autopilot. When you first began driving, it took a lot of thinking to perform the task—grab the keys, look behind the vehicle, get in and crank the car, adjust the mirror, hook your seatbelt, check the gauges, etc. Now, you grab the keys and go! You may be running a little late, talking on the phone, drinking the last bit of coffee while all the time you're driving without thinking about what you have to do. Not that I encourage these things, but it's just an example of how trained we can become in our daily lives.

So many things we do daily are done by the subconscious mind.

So many things we do daily are done by the subconscious mind. Some of those things may have been planted many years ago and are not relevant for today, but they tend to slow you down. Some of those daily activities may persuade you in a way that is not the best choice for the situation.

For example, one of the things my husband realized, as a grown man, was that he would still clean his plate every time he sat down to eat. He never gauged his meals by the sensation of his stomach being satisfied; it was determined by the plate being emptied. He never realized this deep-seated belief was controlling his appetite rather than common sense. His grandmother raised him. It was her past experiences from the Great Depression that created her need for others to eat everything on their plates. Once he accepted this was an unconscious boundary he had also set for himself, he changed it and was able to stop overeating.

Reflection

Can you remember the last time you were kind to yourself? Did that act of kindness include a compliment?

Suggestion

The amazing way you have trained your subconscious mind is something to ponder! Begin believing in the abilities you possess and tell yourself how proud you are for those accomplishments. Smile and relax; you are already enough!

Notes: _____

_____

_____

_____

_____

_____

_____

_____

_____

_____

_____

_____

_____

_____

_____

_____

_____

_____

It All Comes Down To A Choice

_____
_____
_____
_____
_____
_____
_____
_____
_____
_____
_____
_____
_____
_____
_____
_____
_____
_____
_____
_____
_____
_____
_____
_____
_____
_____
_____
_____
_____

9. SLAYING MY GIANT

Now that we have established a few mile markers in our journey together, allow me to bring you to a conclusive point in the story concerning my Dad. I named the chapter, "Slaying My Giant" as this situation received a form of closure for me. During this extended episode, there were times I wondered if I would ever see my Dad again. Of course, there were many questions attached to that one question. Many nights I would lie in bed and imagine scenarios of how it might be. My first few mental screenplays included anger. So many questions I wanted to ask him. Mostly, I needed him to explain why he made the choices he did. How could he just walk out of my life? He knew I thought he hung the moon just for me. My Daddy was my hero. Tears flowed.

As time passed, the nights offered fewer questions as I resolved within my heart that we would never see each other face to face again. Those screenplays held the empty sadness of letting go. The anger had morphed into a feeling of great loss as I missed him dearly. It was worse than death!

> I had finally reached the point where I could talk about him without crying.

Eventually, he rarely crossed my mind. I had finally reached the point where I could talk about him without crying. I knew then my heart had been healed. I was going to be okay, or should I say I had high hopes anyway.

One of the realities of living in a small town is the lack of strangers. Most people know everyone, or at least they know someone who knows everyone! More times than I care to mention, there were things repeated to me by others who knew both my dad and me. Honestly, I do not think anyone had ill intentions; it was just the nature of the small town in which we had both lived. Mostly their remarks were questions from their curious minds. I would kindly respond with a simple yes or no, with little detail, but I never elaborated on the truth—simply because I knew it was not necessary to defend myself. It had lost its importance.

So life carried on. I buried the past, gently laid a blanket over my memories, and bought myself flowers. Everything was going as planned. No speed bumps in the road. No brick walls. No short piers to walk off of. Oh yes, my life was moving right along with no interruptions. That was until the day my aunt was hospitalized. She held on for almost two weeks but eventually succumbed to her illness. She moved to heaven.

My aunt's children, cousins whom I dearly love, asked if I would speak at their mom's funeral.

Bam! There it was. Reality hit me right between my eyes. Dad, her brother, would be there. How would I handle seeing Daddy face to face after eight long years? What was it going to be like to look into his eyes? Could I do that? Thinking of my aunt who loved me dearly, I told them I would be honored.

That night while lying in bed, I questioned my decision. There must have been close to a thousand questions playing basketball inside my head. Funny thing though, it seemed there were no cheerleaders on my side of the court that game! Regardless, I wanted to honor the sincere wishes of my cousins. I knew I had to do this for them and my aunt.

During the basketball game in my head, I purposely double-dribbled and surrendered the ball. The whistle blew, and there was silence. At that moment, I heard the voice of the Lord tenderly tell me I had not completely forgiven my Dad. I was quite shocked at that statement! Surely there was no unforgiveness left in my heart. I pondered the possibility for a moment, knowing deep inside it was true. With closed eyes, head bowed, and heart wide open, I surrendered and released all the hurt and pain which I had been holding and silently clinging to. At that moment, I felt the final release of all the incidents that were only covered in a thin layer of soil. They only appeared to be buried.

The freedom and peace overshadowed me as I completely forgave my Dad, and I wept. This time the tears were not from pain; they were tears of joy. I was at last free.

The day of the funeral arrived. I knew I had to face my giant head on. As my Dad walked past me, I called to him. He either did not hear me or chose to ignore my greeting. I called out to him a second time. Our eyes met and I said, "Hello, Daddy." He didn't speak but he nodded his head and kept walking.

> At that moment, my giant came tumbling down and great was its fall!

Supernatural peace flooded me at that moment, and my heart filled with incredible contentment. At that moment, my giant came tumbling down and great was its fall!

As I mentioned in the Introduction, the defining factor through each season of this journey was forgiveness. Each episode required me to open my heart and be real with myself. Was it possible to let the pain go? How big was my "want to"? There were decisions I had to make. Each choice had a consequence. Ultimately, I chose to forgive as well as forget the pain. The consequences of that decision have been the best thing ever! No longer am I held back—or held down.

If you have not forgiven those who caused you pain, please reconsider that decision.

If the pain was created by no fault of your own, please release it. It served its purpose. Open the door to the cage and set it free; in doing so, you will experience the same freedom. It is beautiful.

Get out of the past and celebrate each day as you begin to realize how heavy that burden of pain truly is.

The weight is not intended to be upon your shoulders. You're simply not big enough to carry such a heavy load.

It is past time to slay your giant and walk, NO! RUN to the other side of your pain!

Reflection

Will you take a moment and ask yourself if you are still unable to forgive the person you thought about at the end of Chapter one?

Suggestion

The unforgiveness you may still be clinging to has a bitter end. Forgiveness doesn't mean everything is okay. It means you choose to free yourself from the torture that unforgiveness can produce. Set your heart free and live again. Untangle yourself from the cords that bind. A beautiful future awaits you!

Notes: _____

_____

_____

_____

_____

_____

_____

_____

_____

_____

_____

_____

_____

_____

_____

_____

_____

Slaying My Giant

_____
_____
_____
_____
_____
_____
_____
_____
_____
_____
_____
_____
_____
_____
_____
_____
_____
_____
_____
_____
_____
_____
_____
_____
_____
_____
_____
_____

10. WHERE TO NOW?

Throughout this book, I have chosen to save the last chapter for what I feel is the best part of my life. Hopefully, it will become the best chapter in your life story as well. I want to become very real with you at this point and talk to you about my very best friend. Without Him, I realize I could not have conquered the situations in my own life.

Apart from Him, I can do nothing.

Please open your heart and take a walk with me.

It's been a journey unlike any I have ever experienced. There has been laughter, there have been tears, but nonetheless, it has changed my life forever. The search for God's presence is the greatest adventure known to man.

During my life, there have been many obstacles and setbacks. These obstacles and setbacks have sometimes made me wonder how I even survived the process. When I reflect back, I am amazed at how strongly the hand of God has kept me safe. Over the years, there were many times when I felt like giving up, especially when every-thing I had set my heart on failed. I had no answers. I was seeking God as to the reasons why, but only casual-ly seeking. Little did I know or understand that all the while He was speaking to my heart, but I was too busy to listen. I found it easier to blame someone else for my mistakes. Sometimes that included blaming God.

To know about God and to truly know God is as differ-ent as man and woman. He is all things to us but will go only as far as we allow Him to go in our lives. I played games with Him for many years, but praise His holy name; it is a game that is best lost.

> **The pain of dying to self is actually not pain at all once the process begins.**

The pain of dying to self is actually not pain at all once the process begins. The Refiner's fire may burn the pride of man for a season; the intensity de-pends on our willingness to confront the old man.

Saying goodbye to the old man is unfamiliar ground. Our flesh just doesn't want to give in to obedience; it is unnatural for many of us. But there is a level we can attain where the spirit man becomes the dominant part of our being.

Where being obedient used to cause us to wrestle on the inside, quite the contrary will take place once we have been in the presence of Almighty God.

The "dying to one's self" was one part of being a Chris-tian that I did not want to go through. I was selfish and self-centered and fought to be on top; little did I know that it was far from the best position to have. I called myself strong, not giving in to this self-made image of weakness. It required opening my heart a little to those around me, and I did not want any part of that.

The assumption of opening my heart was that I would become gullible and be taken advantage of. Many years ago, I had determined that no one would ever take advantage of me again. The exterior was tough and sharp; the interior was tender and frightened. How could I ever allow anyone to see that part of me? There was an image I had to portray, and I learned how to do it very well.

If I had to explain to you where the process began, I would most likely be at a loss for words. It amazes me when someone is able to give you the date and time they were born again. Thinking back, the experiences I have had during my relationship with Yeshua-Jesus just seemed to have always been a part of my life.

No dates to remember, not even really sure of the year I committed my life to God, but I have very vivid memories of adventures with Him. Sadly, I also have memories of adventures without Him. Oh, He was always there; I just became very good at ignoring Him. Those are times I would rather forget, put behind me as Paul said to do in Philippians 3:13, but I must also acknowledge them as being part of the molding process to get me where I am today.

It is so wonderful to serve the risen Savior and to know that He is as close as His name. He lives on the inside of me, and I am in Him. What a phenomenal thought; the maker of heaven and earth lives on the inside of me. The

God who spoke this world into existence, yet created man with His own two hands...

He formed and fashioned us in His image. We actually look like our heavenly Father! He must have eyes to see, ears to hear, a nose to smell, fingers that move, and toes that wiggle. I imagine He even has a ticklish spot. I would think it would be somewhere close to His heart. Have you ever wondered how many times we, as His children, brush against that certain spot? I know He laughs because the Bible states that "a merry heart doeth good like a medicine" (Proverbs 17:22).

~ THE PRICE FOR SIN ~

Living each day to its fullest has been an easy way of putting words into fashion. Some days we feel like running and dancing; other days we choose to hide inside of this shell we call self. When I look back over the years of my life, I feel so many of them have been wasted. Mistakes I have made come back to haunt me when I least expect them to.

It is good to recall past victories given to us by God, but it is not edifying, nor wise, to reflect on those mistakes that have caused us pain and grief. We can always learn from many of our mistakes. Hopefully, we apply the wisdom we learned from past experiences; however, dwelling on the mistakes will only continue to keep us held captive by the past.

There were times during my walk with the Lord when I was presented with an opportunity to slip back into sin.

Occasionally I would bring a small piece of it into my future. The end result was heartache and feeling separated from God.

Although I had full knowledge of the little dab of sin I was getting into, I made the choice to ignore the sweet voice of the Holy Spirit each time He attempted to speak to my heart. Slowly, as I allowed myself to tiptoe around the bush, the sin became a little more comfortable with each step I took. Finally, after several months of being in this comfort zone I had created for myself, I was totally out of touch with my Master—certainly not by His choosing, but rather mine.

The joy of the Lord was gone from my life, thus my strength had diminished. Day after day, my spirit cried out to repent and return to the God of my salvation, but the sin had gotten too comfortable for me to turn my back on it and walk away as I knew to do.

> The joy of the Lord was gone from my life, thus my strength had diminished.

Had I only listened and applied the teachings I had learned from the word of God, I would have completely avoided the heartache. I had no one to blame but myself. There I was again: hurt, angry, confused, empty, and too ashamed to give it to the Lord. In a matter of about six months, I lost all desire to attend church, to read His word, and I even stopped teaching the Bible study I was conducting at my home. I could not even pray because of the guilt and shame I felt deep inside myself. I was truly a miserable individual.

Being lost and feeling separated from my heavenly Father was devastating. His hand never withdrew from reaching out to me. His voice never stopped calling my name. His wisdom never stopped speaking to my heart, and His love for me never grew cold and distant. He longed for me to turn back to Him. Patiently, He waited for me to call His name. Ever so sweetly, He dealt with my heart until the unconditional love of God swept me off my feet and back into His arms.

The awareness of my need for Him exploded on the inside of me as the stars penetrate the darkness of night. Unconditional love, so easily said yet so difficult to accept. I asked myself: Why? Why would God still love me after I let Him down? Why would He forgive me after I knowingly entered into sin? How could He love me after all the mistakes I have made? How could He use someone like me to help others find their way into His arms where they belong?

There it was again, unconditional love. God IS love. He is the fullness of every definition of love. We are His creation made by His own hands, and He is so proud of us. He looks upon us through the precious blood of Christ Jesus; He has clothed us in His righteousness.

Yes indeed, He sent His only Son to die on the cross for us. I am so humbled when I think about Him and His Ultimate Sacrifice! Knowing I would make mistakes even after He saved me, yet He drew me to Himself anyway. He knew I would dabble with sin and walk away from Him. He knew I would mess up so many things in my life, but He loved me enough to die for me! Even if I had been the only person who needed saving. How can I say "Thank You," heavenly Father?

~ PANNING FOR GOLD ~

This journey, as I so affectionately call it, has been an incredible experience that has touched every area of my life and my heart. God has given us so many wonderful nuggets in His word. Yeshua-Jesus is the Word, and the Word is spirit, and it is truth (John 4:24). We can't always understand it with our physical senses.

We must dig into the Word with our spiritual senses to find the nuggets. That is how the Word of God is designed. To know His Word is to know Him! It is like panning for gold or mining for silver. Buried amidst the murky river bottom or hidden beneath layers of rock lies all the answers to man's questions.

Dig a little deeper, shake a little harder, don't give up, one more strike of the pickaxe, one more shake of the sieve, and the glitter of the gold nuggets are exposed. There it is, the reward for our labor, glistening in the midst of the debris.

Although life can shake us at times, we, like the sieve of muddy mess of panning for gold, can come out glistening! As the more vigorously the sieve is jiggled, the more the debris falls off and the golden nuggets suddenly appear! Our hearts can also resemble the rocks if we do not guard them with all diligence as reminded in Proverbs 4:23.

On my journey returning to the love of God, I have noticed that my heart has made so many wonderful changes. Where it used to be that hard, thick rock, it has now been transformed by the love of God. Piece by piece, as His word chipped away the layers, I discovered a softness in the center that I had lost somewhere along my way in life. Kind of reminded me of a Tootsie Roll Pop...although I could be sweet on the outside, I was very hard. Yet much to my surprise, there, hidden in the center, was that softness!

~ SIMPLY BECAUSE HE LOVES US ~

It is so amazing how God will use day-to-day situations in our lives to get our attention. From the simple things of life to the most complex, His hand is always leading us. His love is always drawing us. Look, there, see that flower? It was fashioned by God. See it dancing in the breeze as though it were happy? Feel that very breeze brush across your face, and as it whispers, listen very closely and you can hear our Father saying, "I love you."

He fashioned the birds and dressed them in bright colors for our pleasure. The sky is blue, the clouds are white, and the grass is green—colors of many different shades, leaves of many different shapes. Then there are sounds, each distinct in its own way. All of this, He did for our pleasure, simply because He loves us.

Yeshua-Jesus said in Hebrews 13:5, He would never leave us nor forsake us. People will walk in and out of our lives with no regrets, but I have found that Yeshua-Jesus will always be there to help pick up the pieces and mend any brokenness within us, if we will trust our heart to Him. Unconditional love—are we capable of such a requirement? Without a doubt, the answer is yes, praise the Lord!

When God pours out His love upon us, we have the ability to share that love with those whom we have viewed as unlovable. The Bible tells us in Romans 5:5 that the love of God is shed abroad in our hearts. And when we reach the point of realizing we are truly, sincerely, and unconditionally loved by the Creator of heaven and earth, we can share that love with no hesitation. When we can see people through the eyes of God's love rather than through our own carnal eyes, we will view them as another soul for whom Jesus suffered and died.

> When God pours out His love upon us, we have the ability to share that love with those whom we have viewed as unlovable.

Yeshua-Jesus taught us that a man can have no greater love than to lay down his life for another (John 15:13). That is exactly what Jesus did for us. He gave His life so we could spend eternity with Him. The whole purpose of His coming to earth and taking on the form of man was to reconcile us with the Father. He was born in order to die. He was the final and ultimate sacrifice for mankind. We were separated from God because of the fall of Adam, but Yeshua-Jesus became the bridge between us and eternity with God.

~ CRUNCH TIME ~

The Apostle Paul tells us that we must study to show ourselves approved (2 Timothy 2:15). We all know what it means to study. However, I do believe that most people relate it to the crunch before the test! I never enjoyed taking tests when I was in school, but it was necessary in order for me to get the passing grade. In the long run, it became something I valued, and I wished I had taken schooling a little more seriously. I studied just enough to barely get by, and it was almost always at the very last minute.

The difference here is the fact that we were informed of the day the test would be given. We will not have that opportunity when the Lord returns; not even He knows the day nor the hour (Matthew 24:37). Think back just for a moment to one of the many days when a pop quiz was given in school. Remember the panic that tried to set in? What if we had not been listening in class? What if we failed to study the chapter during the week? I wonder if we will experience a sense of the same panic if we are caught unprepared when the Lord returns? I didn't like the feeling I had on the day of a pop quiz when I was not prepared. I choose to answer my Lord with His word when I have to give account for my life; how about you?

How I long for everyone to be as in love with the Lord as I am. I've lived on both sides of the fence. I would not trade my life with Him for anything this world has to offer. Oh, there is counterfeit pleasure and counterfeit happiness, but that doesn't come from God. Remember, anything counterfeit is not real. Only Christ Jesus can fill that longing that is deep within us. We were created to love and worship Him. This world can offer a temporary pleasure, but only Yeshua-Jesus Christ can offer true happiness. Only His cleansing forgiveness can set us free. Only His love can forever fill our voids.

From the conception of time, our heavenly Father has longed to fellowship with His creation. He walked with Adam in the Garden of Eden. God created this garden especially for him to dwell in forever. He created a paradise for mankind to enjoy, but mankind gave it away. Fellowship with our heavenly Father was broken. One act of disobedience brought division and separation to all of mankind. The end result...man was put out of this paradise, relationship was changed, and sin entered in. But was that truly the end? With a shout of thanksgiving, I can joyously say NO! Remember, God built a bridge between that great divide; His name is Yeshua the Messiah, Jesus Christ our Lord!

~ INFLUENCE OF PERCEPTION ~

Over the past several years, I've had to re-evaluate most of what I had previously been taught concerning God and who I perceived Him to be. You see, most everything I had learned, prior to my wilderness experience, came from the preconceived interpretations of all my past teachers.

When we have a preconceived idea about something or someone, that perception becomes the lens with which we evaluate the event. As with most of us, our beliefs and interpretations are merely learned until we begin to see the kingdom of God through the lens of relationship with our Heavenly Father!

I was unconsciously being fashioned into the image of the teacher's personal beliefs.

Although much of what I had been taught had helped mold me, I realized it rarely molded me into the image of who Father God was revealing Himself to be. He was instead being shaped into a character of the perceived ideas of another person's interpretation of God. I was unconsciously being fashioned into the image of the teacher's personal beliefs.

Let me give you an example: In the past, I had read the Bible through the eyes of fire and brimstone... or, my then perceived image of God. He was always angry when I slipped; always waiting to lean over the edge of heaven and zap me with a lightning bolt! I worked very hard to earn His approval; therefore, His love for me would increase as long as I could keep Him happy, correct? Wrong! Seems I was mostly motivated out of fear because I didn't want to go to hell, not because I longed to please Him.

Reflecting back, I can remember there has always been some type of Christian influence in my life—from fond childhood memories of my Granny slipping me a Kraft caramel during church service, to friends whom my heavenly Father placed in my path to encourage and love me.

Jesus would always find a way to remind me of His un-
ending love, but it was difficult for me to accept that
truth. Besides, didn't I read somewhere in the Bible
about a two-edged sword? Fear of His anger would keep
me at a distance if I felt I had failed Him. Over the years,
my perception had been formed by what I had been
taught, and this became a core belief of who I thought
God to be. But, I never really knew Him—I only knew
the traditions of men I had been taught.

Life for me became rituals which became my religion.
If I didn't pray for 30 minutes each morning or read
through the Bible once a year, I was not going to make
it to heaven. My list of Do's and Don'ts became overwhelming. I could relate to what Jesus said when He
talked about traditions in Mark chapter 7! Please, don't
take me wrongly, I fully agree with praying and reading
the Bible! Actually, we are told to study to show ourselves approved (2 Tim 2:15). Personally, I feel that's the
beginning of deep revelation and relationship. I'm just
simply reminding us to examine the motivation behind
our efforts; is it tradition, fear, or perfect love?

Sadly, I spent many years trying to become good enough
to earn my place in heaven. This resulted in effort after
silly effort of nothing other than dead works. No matter how hard we try, we can never earn our salvation; it
comes only through Jesus as a gift of Papa God's unconditional love (John 3:16).

Thankfully, the day finally came when I removed my
angry-colored glasses. A personal relationship with my
heavenly Father started forming. I began to see Him
through the perception of adoration! I put on my

love-colored glasses and began to view Him through much different lenses!

His word became a personal love letter to me, written by the blood of Jesus. Compassion filled each page. Love flowed effortlessly through my eyes into my heart. I truly became His beloved! I finally got it...revelation of John...listening to the very heartbeat of Yeshua-Jesus as his head leaned against the Master's chest.

Love, pure love, unlike anything I had ever experienced. I was gently swept away by the current of Living Water into the heart of 'Everlasting Love'! God is love (1 John 4:16).

As Graham Cooke says:

> *There is nothing you can do to make the Lord love you more. There is also nothing you can do that would make Him love you less. He loves you because He loves you, because He loves you, because He loves you, because He loves you! Because that is what He is like. It is His nature to love and you will always be the beloved, and His love is unchanging. He loves you 100%. He won't love you any better when you become better. He loves you 100% right now..."*

Now, will you take a moment and observe your perception of Father God? Is He 'Abba' or 'Angry'? Is He 'Fire and Brimstone' or does He give you the absolute best hugs? If you will allow yourself to be loved, you, too, will begin to see your Heavenly Father through your new pair of love glasses! It's never too late to change your perception.

~ COMPASSION BORN OF LOVE ~

Following is my paraphrase of a story in the Bible about a woman who was caught in the act of adultery (John 8:3-11). Any sin can be the focal point, but the outcome will always be the same with Yeshua-Jesus. As you read, put yourself and your sin in this woman's place and experience this along with her.

❧

No. Please. Not there. Please don't make me go in front of all those people. I've said I am sorry. I've begged for forgiveness. Please...

Gathering all the strength I can, I resist the Pharisee. I feel his calloused hand tighten on my arm. He angrily pulls me as he shoves through the gathered crowd. With one last thrust, he propels me into the middle of the people. I fall to my knees, my head hung low.

I have never felt as humiliated as I do at this moment. Everyone will know what I've done. The truth will be told—my sin exposed. There's no place to hide, no place to cover my shame. I'm caught and must face the consequences. But I'm afraid. I don't think I can handle my punishment. I know I deserve it, but I'm frightened!

Suddenly, a loud voice pierces the curious whispers of the crowd. "Teacher, this woman was caught in adultery, in the very act."

Oh, there it is; I bow lower to the ground wishing for some place to hide. What have I done? Why did I not resist the temptation? Why did I think I might finally find love in the arms of that man? How foolish I've been. And now I must die.

Again he cries out, "Moses, in the law, commanded us that such should be stoned. But, what do You say, Teacher?"

A hush falls over the crowd. All I can hear at that moment is the pounding of my heart. I think, "Who is this Teacher? Who has so much authority that the crowd silences themselves in anticipation of His answer?" I want to look up, but dare not raise my head.

Silence.

Waiting.

Did the Teacher not hear the angry voice? Is he so ashamed of what I did that he needs to weigh out my punishment? Is he as angry as the Pharisees who have gathered here?

Again, the man cries out to the Teacher, "What shall we do with her?" As I wait, I wipe the tears from my face and stare at my bare feet. A gentle voice breaks the silence. It's the most beautiful voice I've ever heard. He answers, "He who is without sin among you, let him throw the first stone."

Oh no, please. My heart beats faster. My breathing increases. Oh God, I am so sorry; forgive me. Please let me die quickly. Please let the first stone take my life. I wrap my arms tightly around my stomach as I wait for the stone to strike me. I'm not ready to die, but I deserve what I receive. Fear grips me. I freeze in anticipation. My life begins to replay in my mind. How very differently I would do things if given another chance. So many wrongs I would make right if I could go back.

Listen...there it is again, that beautiful voice. Wait, is he speaking to me? "Woman," he says, "Where are those accusers of yours? Has no one condemned you?" I can hardly believe what I'm hearing! I slowly lift my head, wipe my tears once more, and glance around. There's no one with me except the Teacher. Where did they go? What has just happened? We are alone.

I look toward him and answer, "No one, Lord." And the Teacher says to me, "Neither do I condemn you; go and sin no more."

With that, I gaze into his eyes; I'm overwhelmed with compassion and love. Never have I felt so much love from anyone. Instantly, my heart is captured and I have no desire to sin again.

For the first time in my life, I know what it feels like to be loved, truly loved. I need look no further. My sins are forgiven; I am not condemned. I am loved completely by the one called Teacher. Surely, He is the Messiah, the Son of the Living God! I have looked into the eyes of Love.

THANK YOU, LORD JESUS!

~ ONE FINAL QUESTION ~

As we come to the end of this book, there is one final question I'd like to ask you—have you ever given your heart to Yeshua-Jesus? Or maybe you have in the past but your love has grown cold? If you don't have a personal relationship with Christ, I'd love to help you develop one. It all begins in your heart with the decision that you want to know Him. Just calling on His name will bring you into His presence. I've heard it said He is as close as His name! Here is a short prayer to get you on your way into the adventure of a lifetime and the promise of eternity!

"Yeshua, Christ Jesus, I want to know You—not just know about You but to know You in my heart as my Lord and Savior. I'm asking You to come live within me. I ask for Your forgiveness for the wrong I have done in the past. Wash me with Your blood so I may be clean. I choose to make You Lord of my life.

"Come into my heart and make it Your home, so I can always find You there. I believe Father God raised You from the dead, so thank You for loving me enough to die in my place that I could be saved. I love You! Amen!"

My friend, welcome to the family of God! Let me encourage you to find a gathering place where you can grow in the knowledge of the Word of God. Other believers can be great encouragement for the new adventure you are about to enjoy. Pray and ask the Father to direct you to where you need to be. He will lead you!

I also encourage you to first read the Gospel of John in the New Testament of the Bible. Before you start your walk through the scriptures, invite the Holy Spirit to open your eyes to who Yeshua-Jesus was, and is, and is to come!

God loves you far beyond your comprehension, and I pray you will seek His love with a passion. There truly is no greater feeling in the world than to know Father God loves you... unconditionally!

Thank you for purchasing and reading this book. I pray it is a great source for healing your heart. If you will apply the things I have written within these pages, then pain will eventually depart from you. Always remember you are stronger than the pain and it is not welcomed within you! Joy unthinkable and full of glory will be found on the other side of your pain!

May God bless you always in all ways!

Notes: _____

_____
_____
_____
_____
_____
_____
_____
_____
_____
_____
_____
_____
_____
_____
_____
_____
_____
_____
_____
_____
_____
_____
_____
_____

Where To Now?

_____
_____
_____
_____
_____
_____
_____
_____
_____
_____
_____
_____
_____
_____
_____
_____
_____
_____
_____
_____
_____
_____
_____
_____
_____
_____
_____
_____

The Spirit of the Lord is upon Me, because He has anointed Me to preach the gospel to the poor; He has sent Me to heal the brokenhearted, to proclaim liberty to the captives and recovery of sight to the blind, to set at liberty those who are oppressed; to proclaim the acceptable year of the Lord.

Mark 4:18,19

ABOUT THE AUTHOR:

Terri Jordan is an or-
dained minister of the
gospel, speaker, counsel-
or, and friend. Terri and
her husband, Buzz, live in
a rural community in Ala-
bama within a motorcycle
ride from their daughter,
son-in-law and two amaz-
ing grandchildren.

Together, she and her husband founded and pastored
His Vineyard Church for several years. While Terri may
be soft spoken, the anointing she carries produces power
behind her words. Her gifting to see beyond the obvious
allows her to flow in a prophetic rhythm as she minis-
ters.

Terri has a passion to reach others who have suffered at
the hands of religion and introduce them to a relationship with Yeshua-Jesus. She has tasted and seen that the
Lord is good and longs to share that with those who
may not know God as a loving Father. His love is inde-

scribable, and His mercy exceeds any limitation we face. Terri desires to help people turn their trauma into triumph and their pain into possibilities through knowing who they truly are through Yeshua-Jesus.

Terri Jordan Ministries
P.O. Box 1363
Jackson, AL 36545
terrijordanministries@proton.me

For additional resources please visit:
www.terrijordanministries.org/

www.ingramcontent.com/pod-product-compliance
Lightning Source LLC
LaVergne TN
LVHW051249080426
835513LV00016B/1831